Traditionalism Of Life

REFORMATION TOWARDS RESTORATION

PUBLISHED BY

MINISTER F. IRVING PEARSALL

OUTREACH MINISTRIES
voicemail 732-298-2199

Order this book online at www.trafford.com
or email orders@trafford.com

Most Trafford titles are also available at major online book retailers.

First printing 2010

Scriptures quotations in this book are taken from the King James
Version and the Amplified Bible, by the Lockman Foundation.

This book is not for sale for profit, the publisher however will accept a contribution
or donation to cover the price per book. The cost to the publisher because this book
contains scriptures quoted from god's sacred holy word the bible wherein it is written
"my gospel without charge," 1 Corinthians 9: 16-18; Ecclesiastes: 12:13-14.

So in following what is the acceptable will of God, our purpose
and goals is so that more books can be printed and distributed
worldwide. So that anyone can afford to obtain and read.

Thank you,
The Publisher

Printed in the United States of America.

ISBN: 978-1-4269-5479-5 (sc)
ISBN: 978-1-4269-5480-1 (e)

Library of Congress Control Number: 2011901285

Trafford rev. 04/12/2011

 www.trafford.com

North America & international
toll-free: 1 888 232 4444 (USA & Canada)
phone: 250 383 6864 ♦ fax: 812 355 4082

DEDICATION

In memory of my beloved Mother
Ethel Mariah Pearsall
(1900 - 1976)

INTRODUCTION

The message in this book is a struggle to make real to the believers the hidden prosperity of an almost unknown truth, of the word of God.

The publisher has felt for years that the disciples had a power to which we are utterly strangers, and that this power should belong to the believers.

God has been seeking a solution to this problem and he is waiting for his word to be an unveiling of the hidden truth.

I hope that others will build upon this foundation, and that before the return of our Lord, Christ Jesus, the holy redeemer and savior, the messiah, the anointed one, that a portion at least of the body of believers will be living in the freshness of the power of the Life style of the first Christians, the early Church in Jerusalem. If this book has enlightened you, then pass it on so that others may be comforted and enlightened of this truth.

This is the whole purpose and goal for the publishing of this book, that others will desire and choose to read God's sacred Holy word, the Bible, and to fellowship one to another. 1 John 1:4-10

Let us pray that God will continue to bless America.

Thank You,
The Publisher

ABOUT THE PUBLISHER. . .
MINISTER F. IRVING PEARSALL

I was born in Beaufort, N.C. in 1939 and I received my early training there, before moving to New Jersey in my early teens where I completed my early education. My brother, David and I owned and operated an offset printing business in Newark, NJ for over thirty years. I also taught young vocational students just entering the graphic arts field for work in the printing trades in NYC.

In 1994 I retired and moved to Oakland, Ca. Through the loving kindness of God I was led to Calvary Christian Center in Sacramento, Ca. and under the teaching Ministries of Pastor, Dr. Phillip G. Goudeaux, Minister and teacher, Emmet Lewis, the word of God entered into my heart and mind, I became intensely inspired and enlightened. God's word put a strong desire in me and I became a Guest Speaking Outreach Minister, in hope of inspiring Family members and others to read Gods Sacred Holy Word, the Bible.

One might ask or think, what is my belief and faith as an Outreach Guest Speaking Minister. 'I true fully and rightfully can say that I am a *'Fundamentalist'* one who believes in the *'Infallibility'* of the Holy Bible, the words that come from the mind of God, according to it's exact meaning, that has not been found void, for over two thousand years. The greatest and most read published book in the world. People everywhere in life from every walk and station from every town, city, state and nation have given me so many tangible and intangible things so dear, I couldn't begin to count them all or even make them clear, I only know I owe so much to God, the Creator, and his *Loving kindness*, and when I put my thoughts in words, it's just a way of sharing a thankful heart, a heart much like your own, for nothing that I think or write is mine and mine alone., so if you find some enlightenment and beauty in any word or line it's just your soul *'Reflection in Harmony" (Peace) with mine.*

Min. F. Irving Pearsall

𝔗𝔯𝔞𝔡𝔦𝔱𝔦𝔬𝔫𝔞𝔩𝔦𝔰𝔪 𝔒𝔣 𝔏𝔦𝔣𝔢

REFORMATION TOWARDS RESTORATION

TO WALK IN THE LIGHT IN MIND AND CHARACTER

"And these things write we unto you, that your joy may be full. This then is the message which we have heard of him, and declare unto you, that *God is Light*, and in him is no darkness at all. If we say that we have fellowship with him, and walk in darkness we lie, and do not the truth; but if we walk in the *Light*, as he is in the *Light*, we have *Fellowship one with another*, and the blood of Jesus Christ his Son cleanseth us from all sin.

If we say that we have no sin, we deceive ourselves, and the *truth* it not in us. If we *Confess* our *sins*, he is faithful and just to *Forgive* us our sins, and to *cleanse us* from all unrighteousness.

If we say that we have not *sinned*, we make him a liar, and his word is not in us. (Our Hearts)"

First John 1:4-10

CONTENTS

PART ONE

TRANSITION

"He shall not alter it, nor change it, a good for a bad, or a bad for a good: and if he shall at all change beast for beast, then it and the exchange thereof shall be holy."
Leviticus 27: 10

There is nothing new in saying that we live in an age of transition. Someone has facetiously said that when Adam and Eve were out of the Garden of Eden, Adam turned to Eve and said, "My Dear, this is an age of *transition*."

The oldest known bit of writing in the world is a piece of papyrus in a Constantinople museum. A species of Egyptian reed, a musical instrument to vibrate in a current of air from which the ancients made paper, a manuscript. On it is written; Alas, and exclamation expressive of unhappiness, sorrow, pity or like emotions. Times are not what they used to be, children no longer obey their parents and everyone wants to write a book. We are suffering from *transition*.

The change effected or the period of time during which the change takes place I feel, that we are suffering from it as one does from measles. *Transition* does seem to be as recurring as measles and ever generation suffers, nevertheless, no one can get in the midst of this flowing passing current of this age, without feeling that the thoughts and ideas and tendencies flowing there are not ripples on the surface, but something that is changing the whole fundamental outlook on life. We are in the throes, agony, great *distress of mind, of a passing from* facts *Traditionalism of Life* based upon the authority of facts, of truth, of experiences, this whole tendency sends life straight to the door of our government and the Christian Church, and there it stands waiting for some clear word of *Guidance*, some note of certain experience of *God*, of the way to live of power over evil and self, of being victorious, successful in human living, of worldwide Godly brotherhood. Can our government and the churches speak these words out of the depths of its own radiant sense of God, and out of its own experience of victory in life out of its deep sense of sureness amid a world of crushing change?

I wish I could answer that with a clear ring "yes" but by close study and intimate knowledge with hundreds of ministers and Gods sacred holy word of many years, with the general church life in the east and west, I am compel to say that our government and the church is largely unprepared for this hour. If the whole demand for experience heads us straight towards Pentecost, candor compels me to say that the Church is not *living in Pentecost*. It is living between *Easter and Pentecost.*

Easter stands for life wrought out, greatly honored decorative. Pentecost stands for *Life* appropriated, lived to its *fullest*, unafraid and clearly and powerfully witnessing to an adequate way of human living. The church stands *hesitant* between the two. Hesitant, hence comparatively impotent. Something big has dawned on its thinking *Christ* has lived, taught, died and risen again and has *Commissioned* the church with the amazing *Good News*, but something has yet to dawn in the structural makeup, and temper of the

Life of the Church, Pentecost. Easter has dawned; Pentecost has not, Pentecost, a Jewish holiday, the fiftieth day after the second day of Passover, also a Christian holiday, the Seventh Sunday after Easter, in memory of speaking in tongues, and theory of speaking in tongues, and full filling of the Holy Spirit by the Apostles. (Acts 2: 1)

"And when the day of Pentecost was fully come, they were all with one accord in one place, and suddenly there came a sound from Heaven as of a rushing mighty wind, and it filled all the house where they were sitting, and there appeared unto them cloven tongues filled with the 'Holy Spirit' and began to speak with other tongues, as the Spirit gave them utterance, and there were dwelling at Jerusalem Jews, devout men out of every nation under Heaven." (Pentecost an actual celebrated holiday, yet not celebrated.) If the church would move up from that between-state to Pentecost, nothing could stop it--, Nothing! Now it is stopping itself by its own ponderous machinery.

THE DAY OF PENTECOST, THE COMING OF THE HOLY SPIRIT

Seven weeks had gone by since Jesus death and resurrection, and the Day of Pentecost had now arrived. As the believers met together that day, suddenly there was a sound like the roaring of a mighty windstorm in the skies about them and it filled the house where they were meeting.

Then what looked like flames or tongues of fire appeared and settled on their heads.

And everyone present was filled with the HOLY SPIRIT and began speaking in languages they didn't know, for the Holy Spirit gave them this ability.

Many godly Jews were in Jerusalem that day for The Religious CELEBRATIONS, HAVING arrived from many Nations.

And when they heard the roaring in the sky above the house, CROWDS came running to see what it was all about, and were stunned to hear their own languages being spoken by the Disciples.

How can this be' they exclaimed,' for these men are all from Galilee, and yet we hear them speaking all the native languages of the lands where we were born. Here we are-Parthians, Medes, Elamites men from MESOPOTAMIA, JUDEA, CAPPADOCIA, PONTUS, AUSIA, PHRYGIA, PAMPHYLIA, EGYPT. The Cyrene language area of LIBYA, visitors from ROME—both Jews and Jewish converts, proselytes convert believers, (to-JUDAISM) from other RELIGIONS.

Cretans, and Arabians. And we all hear them speaking in our native tongues (and) telling of) THE MIGHTY MIRACLES WORKS OF GOD.

They stood there amazed and perplexed, what can this mean, they asked each other.

But others in the crowd were mocking, they're drunk, that's all, they said. Then Peter stepped forward with the Eleven Apostles, and shouted to the crowd, "LISTEN, all of you, visitors and residents of JERUSALEM alike, some of you are saying these men are drunk, it isn't true, it's much to early for that, People don't get drunk by 9 A.M., WHAT YOU SEE this morning was predicted CENTURIES AGO by the Prophet JOEL – In the LAST DAYS, "GOD SAID I WILL POUR OUT MY HOLY SPIRIT UPON ALL MANKIND.

And your sons and daughters shall Prophesy, and your young men shall see visions and your old men dream dreams.

Yes the HOLY SPIRIT shall come upon all my SERVANTS, MEN and WOMAN alike, and they shall PROPHESY.

And I will cause strange Demonstrations in the Heavens and on the Earth, Blood and fire and clouds of smoke, The sun shall turn black and the moon Blood red before that awesome DAY OF THE LORD arrives.

But ANYONE who ask for MERCY from the LORD, shall have it and shall be SAVED.

Acts 2:1-21

PART TWO

PENTECOST IS NOT
A LIVING FACT WITH US

The Holy Spirit given to Gentile believers
"While Peter yet spoke these words, the Holy Ghost fell on all
them which heard the word."
Acts 10:44

Whenever we have been troubled in conscience about our spiritual impatience we have added a new wheel, or commission, a new plan, a new committee, and a larger building, or program and in the end we have found that we have added one more wheel, but with little or no power to run the old or the new. We become busy devastatingly busy—turning old and new wheels by hand power, by sheer hand power instead of lighting central fires. So much of this is forced, nerve wearing, instead of spontaneous healing, *"Pentecost is not a living fact with us."* Hence we worship machinery instead of winning and saving souls. *Proverbs 11:30* as it is written, thus saith the Lord, *"The fruit of the righteous is a tree of life: and he that winneth souls is wise."*

A minister friend told me of a traveling experience he had in the mountains of Lake Tahoe, NV, caught in a snow storm, on one of the worst winding roads in the state of Nevada, the driver of the automobile had never driven in such a high elevation before and it happened that on his first trip the previous day he had almost gone over one of those terrifying precipitous cliffs. He was nervous, so before starting back he came around in front of the engine and stood with folded hands saying his prayers to the machine.

That done, he started off, but had not gone far when the engine began to overheat. There was no water in the radiator! This was remedied, but many miles from his destination the machine stopped while going up a hill. There was no gas in the tank! There he stayed until rescued. The driver said his prayers to the machine, but put no water in the radiator, and no gas in the tank. He ran on left-overs- and stopped. How often we worship the machinery of our Ecclesiasticisms, devotion to principles, forms, and tradition of the world. *Colossians 2: 8 "Beware lest any man spoil you through philosophy and vain deceit, after the tradition of men after the rudiments of the world, and not after Christ."* Depending on left overs that have come down to us from the sacrifices of our fathers, neglect the sources of power, and then stop dead: as it is written, thus saith the Lord. Then said Jesus unto his disciples. "If any man serve me, let him follow me; and where I am there shall also my servant be; if any man serve me, him will my Father honour." John 12:26. *Imagine the Early Church with Pentecost Eliminated;* Imagine these men going out to interpret that wonderful message, but themselves not inwardly corresponding with the message: that gap would have been their loss of that power and of movement. *Pentecost* made the men and the message one, they forfeit their power. We cannot imagine the church with *Pentecost Eliminated.* For there would have been no Church. Here the church was Born. True, there had been the period of potential, for this holy thing lay within the womb of the purpose of God and was nourished by the life and teaching of Christ: The cross was the birth-pain; Easter heralded the coming birth, but *Pentecost was the Birthday*. On that day was born the *New Humanity*. A new type of human being came into existence as different from ordinary humanity, as ordinary humanity is, different from the animals. The qualities of compassion, kindness and sympathy, and moral feelings, that makes us enter into the distresses, suffering, of others, that are in great physical and mental pain. But suppose for a moment there had been no *Pentecost*, the situation would have been impossible for them. Here were men *commissioned to proclaim a crucified Christ Jesus as Savior, Master, and Messiah.* They were to replace the present world order with a new world order, *The Kingdom Of God, and all this in face of a deep hostility with their pre-Pentecost resources, an impossible task.*

* * *

PART THREE

FEAR

*"Humanity is always meeting obstacles. All Honor To the men
who do not fear obstacles, but push them aside and press on."*
Philippians 3:14

Without this *Inner transformation and moral re-enforcement*,
we would expect to find them just where we do find them; it
was evening on that day, the first day of the week when the
doors were shut, where the disciples were assembled for *fear
of the Jews."* A church behind closed doors: living between
Easter and Pentecost is always behind closed doors.

They had ringing in their ears the most gracious word
that ever broke into human life *The Gospel;* they had seen
the most perfect exhibition of living that this planet has
known—*His Life;* they had witnessed earth's most terrific
and decisive moral struggle, his death, they had found their
sadness turned into joy over the most transforming and
astonishing fact in history, *His Resurrection*, they had seen
wounds that would heal wounds, and death that would
banish death, a resurrection that would raise a world into
a New Life, they had looked into that face, so tender, so
triumphant, and had heard him commission them to go share

this with the world, Matthew 28:19-20. "Go ye therefore, and teach all nations, baptizing them in the name of the Father, and Son, and of the *Holy Ghost:* teaching them to observe all things, whatsoever I have commanded you; and Lo, I am with you always, even unto the end of the world. A-men." And what had they done? They had shut themselves up behind closed doors for fear they had the message The World Needed and Awaited, the one message that would Heal, the sin-hurt of the world and yet that message was shut up behind closed doors. The only power that could and did get them out from behind closed doors and loose them and their message upon the world was *Pentecost.* It was not enough for them to see him and to hear him say *"Peace be unto you; as my Father hath sent me, even so I send you."* John 20:21-23. His presence and his commission were not enough, for a week later we find them still behind closed doors. His assurance and his commission did not get them out, only *Pentecost got them out.* Acts 2:1-5. "And when the day of Pentecost was fully come, they were all with one accord in one place." "And suddenly there came a sound from heaven as of a rushing mighty wind, and it filled all the house where they were sitting. And there appeared unto them cloven tongues like as of fire, and it sat upon each of them. And they were all filled with the *Holy Spirit*, and began to speak with other tongues, as the spirit gave them utterance. And there were dwelling at Jerusalem, Jews, *Devout Men, of every Nation Under Heaven."* For up to *Pentecost* the whole thing was on the outside of them, objective, something spoken, acted before them, it wasn't in them at *Pentecost* this gospel came within them, became identical with them—what they had heard and seen and what they were became one, hence they became irresistible of a mighty passion. In Jerusalem the early Christians showed forth to all who would see what life in the new Kingdom of God was meant to be. Christ had told his followers that fraternal love would set them off as His disciples. "By this will all men know that you are my disciples if you have love for one another." (John 13:35) The early Christians lived in so great mutual charity that pagans observing them commented in amazement, "See how these Christians love one another."

This was especially true of the very first Christians in Jerusalem. "And all who believed were together and held all things in common, and would sell their possessions and goods and distribute them among all according as anyone had need." (Acts 2:44-45)

Church came to life, so to speak, as the Holy Spirit came down upon the Apostles and entered into the depths of their being. The Spirit of God filled the Church when he came into it on Pentecost. Since that day he has continued to abide in the Church and He will do so until the end of time. In the Church the Holy Spirit not only dwells, but acts. He guides the Mystical Body of Christ in the way of holiness and truth. Coming down upon the Apostles, He set them to carrying out the mission which Christ had given them—to convert all nations. Through the succeeding centuries, He has accompanied and aided their successors, and will do so to the end of time, that they may accomplish their work in each generation: teaching all nations, Baptizing them, and guiding them to live according to the law of God.

The promise of Christ to His Apostles has been fulfilled: "I will ask the Father and he will give you another (Helper) to dwell with you forever, the Spirit of Truth, whom the world cannot receive, because it seeth him not, neither knoweth him, but you shall know him, because he will dwell with you, and be in you." (John 14:16-18)

The church today is behind close doors for Fear. The church has often stayed behind closed systems of thought for fear of the scientist, afraid that the scientist will explain away things that have become precious to us.

The Gospel record the appearance in human history and within the *Hebrew* nation of the promised *Messiah Jesus Christ*, and tell the wonderful story of his *Manifestation to Israel*, his *Rejection* by that people, his *Crucifixion, Resurrection*, and *Ascension*. The Acts of the Apostles record the descent of the *Holy Spirit*, and the beginning of a new thing in human history, *The Church*. The division of the race now becomes threefold—*The Jew, The Gentile, and the Church of God.* Just as Israel is in the foreground from the call of Abram to the resurrection of Christ, so now the *Church* fills the scene from the *second* chapter of Acts to the *fourth* chapter of *Revelation*. The remaining chapters of that book complete the story of *Humanity* and the final triumph of *Christ*. His person as *"God Manifest in the Flesh."* Which constitute the *Gospel.* (1 Timothy 3:16) "And without controversy great is the mystery of *Godliness.* "And God was manifest in the flesh, justified in the *Spirit*, seen of angels, preached unto the *Gentiles*, believed on in the world, received up into *glory."* (To Reunite)

* * *

PART FOUR

FAITH

WHAT IS FAITH?
"It is the confident assurance that what we hope for is going to happen. It is the evidence of things we cannot yet see."
Hebrews 11-1

We clasp our *Faith* to our bosoms to protect it forgetting that our faith does not need protection—it needs *Proclamation*, the act of proclaiming and announcing to the world and member of the Christian Ministry to admit to the ministry of *Priesthood,* if it is real, it is its own protection, if it is not real, then the sooner we find it out the better. Then said *Jesus* unto them; when ye have lifted up the Son of man, then shall ye know that *I* am *He, I* speak these things. And he that sent me is with me; the *Father* hath not left me alone; for *I* do *Always* those things that pleases him. As he spoke these words, many believed on him. Then said *Jesus* to those Jews which believed on him, *If* ye continue in my word, then are ye my *Disciples* indeed: (works of faith and truth) *And ye shall know the truth, and the truth shall make you free.* (John 8:31-32)

There is only one refuge in life and that is in truth and reality. If our *Faith* can be broken, the sooner it is broken the better. So I have my faith and have put it out these years before the non-Christian world and have said; "There it is, brothers; break it, if it can be broken, only the truth can make me free." It is glorious to watch your faith rise out of the stress, resplendent, shinning the brighter the more it is in *"Love"* Faith must work, it must produce, it must be *Visible*, Verbal faith is not enough, mental faith insufficient, true faith must be there, it must inspire action. *Faith* obeys the word. It will not merely hear and not do. *Faith* produces doers. It harbors no prejudice. *Faith and Favoritism* can not coexist. When the *Holy Spirit direct out lives, He will produce, this kind of fruit in us.* "But the fruit of the spirit is *Love, Joy, Peace, Long Suffering, Gentleness, Goodness, "Faith" Meekness, Self-control*, against such there is no law, and they that are *Christ's* have crucified the flesh with the affections and lust. If we live in the spirit, let us also walk in the spirit. Let us not be desirous of vain glory, provoking one another, envying one another." (Galatians 5:22-26) True faith must manifest evidents, by taking part in showing clear to our sight of understanding, to obtain knowledge of through our senses of understanding. So should one think or say that the church is not living in *Pentecost, but living between Easter and Pentecost*, for *Fear*, with little *Faith* or no *Faith* at all." Now it came to pass on a certain day that Jesus went into a ship with his disciples; and he said unto them, let us go over unto the other side of the lake, and they launched *they sailed Jesus fell asleep;* and there came down a storm of wind on the lake; and they were filled with water, and were in jeopardy, and they came to him, and awoke him, saying, Master, Master, we perish, Then Jesus arose, and rebuked the wind and the raging of the water; and they ceased, and there was a calm. And he said unto them *Where is your Faith?* And they being afraid wondered, saying one to another, what manner of man is this? For he commandeth even the winds and water, and they obey him" (Luke 8:22-25) The truth does make us free.

In my hometown as a very young boy, 9 years of age, I saw a monument of Christopher Columbus, whose stature stood upon the top. In front of the base a figure of Liberty—her torch stood on top; on one side of her stood youth looking with eager face toward the dawn; on the other was learning, her face thoughtful, and open book before her; below these figures were strong muscular men pushing at the bow of a boat, depicting the boat of human progress; this whole side of the monument evidently design to show progress. It was all eager, and faced toward the dawn. On another were two men caught in the rope of serpents, one had died, his face was upon his hands, a broken, defeated soul, but the other was putting up a great battle. He was removing the serpent about him and there was a look of hope in his face as he looked toward the rising sun, this side showed the fierce moral struggle that the *God* of this world put before some men to under go. (2 Corinthians 4:1-6)

"Therefore seeing we have this ministry, as we have received mercy, we faint not; but have renounced the hidden things of dishonesty, not walking in craftiness, nor handling the word of *God* deceitfully; but by manifestation of the truth commending ourselves to every mans conscience in the sight of *God*. But if our gospel be hid, it is hid to them that are lost; in whom the *God* of this world hath blinded the minds of them which believe not, lest the light of the glorious gospel of *Christ*, who is the image of *God*. Should shine unto them, for we preach not ourselves, but *Christ Jesus the Lord:* and ourselves your servants for Jesus sake. For *God* who commanded the light to shine out of darkness, hath shined in our hearts, to give the light of the knowledge of the glory of *God in the face of (Jesus Christ).* (2 Corinthians 4:3-6)

On the opposite side was a pagan figure with world in his hand, at the back of the monument, faced toward the setting sun the figure of *Faith*, a palm branch in one hand, an anchor in the other, her face placid and calm, her eyes blind folded. I said to myself, *Faith* what are you doing here, faced toward the setting sun? Why aren't you around on the other side of this monument facing the rising sun? You should be the soul of liberty, the inspiration of youth, the heart of learning, and strength and courage to those men who push the boat of human progress into the future, and *Faith* what are you doing to help those men in their moral struggle as they battle with the Serpents of Passion and Lust too strong for them? And why aren't those eyes blind folded? This is not Faith, this is credulity, belief and trust. Credulity is blind folded, *Faith* is open-eyes, eager to know the *Truth* that shall set men free. No wonder paganism holds that world on the other side. *Faith ceases* to be afraid and looks at life open-eyed and frank, comes around in front and assumes the moral leadership, because *Faith* thinks beyond, experiences beyond, and goes beyond all human life. *In Valparaiso, which means "the vale of Paradise," I saw the beautiful Harbor strewn with the hulks of wrecked ships.* I wondered why there was so much wreckage in this vale of paradise. I was told the harbor, though beautiful is subject to terrific storms which break in from the sea, and that the only safe thing to do in a storm is to weigh anchor and make for the open ocean. Ships hug the safety of the harbor are almost invariably wrecked. Safety comes in the open sea.

If religion hugs its safe harbor and gazes upon its entrancing vales of paradise, the wreckage of the future will be terrible, had I not seen the wreckage of *Faith* in that very vale of paradise. The whole of the intellectuals were to alienate from religion turning to void of interest of life agnosticism, the doctrine that teaches that nothing is known or knowable of the origin of nature of the universe or the creator, except the physical manifestation of phenomena, belief that all we know is what is perceived through the physical senses, blindly groping amid cults that promise a way of life, because the church had impose its authority instead of teaching men to find the authority of truth through a personal relationship with *God the Father, God the Son, and God the Holy Spirit.* The only safety is in the open sea, where we have inward resources that can outride any storm of criticism or any search for reality. The open sea is out home. Our gospel came out of life and it speaks to life "Faith is not belief in spite of evidence, but life lived in scorn of consequences, "I am afraid of safety, said Paul at dawn when they asked him to flee for safety, both physically and spiritually his inner surety was his safety, but the church today has not realized the fact, so it is in large measure behind closed systems of thought, clamped down hard and fast, for fear of *Thinker and Scientists*. The church is behind closed economic systems, fearing to offend wealthy contributors. Modern life is organized on behalf of those who have and *against* those who *have not*, in an acquisitive society, money is the golden key that unlocks privileges, education, positions, and power. We know in our heart of hearts that this is wrong and un-Christian, it cuts straight across *Christ's Mind*, yet the church is so dependent on that acquisitive society for its economic maintenance that it locks it self behind a closed economic system. We are afraid, so we close the doors. The church is behind closed doors of race exclusiveness for *Fear of losing* and offending contributors, so we fall short of the glory of God, that is to say "To save Souls."

"The Fruit of the *Righteous* is a tree of life; and he that winneth souls, (save) is wise." Proverbs 11:30.

* * *

PART FIVE

THE MESSENGER AND
THE MESSAGE

"I Beheld till the thrones were cast down, and the Ancient of days did sit, whose garment was white as show, and hair of his head like the pure wool: his throne was like the fiery flame, and his wheels as burning fire." Daniel 7:9-Revelation 1:11-20

A new kind of religion has been evolved; the religion of being white, yet our own master *Jesus the Messiah was not white.* A friend made this statement in a public address and a lady came up at the close page and trembling with emotion. Jesus not white! The bottom had dropped out of her religion. I repeated this statement before a group of ministers and a friend at the rear heard an excited and involuntary exclamation came from the lips of a minister, that's a lie *"that's a lie" but it is probably the truth.* We liken Jesus to the modern Jew, who is white, but the modern Jew has been two thousand years or more under cover and has been bleached out to see the former Jew of that day, we must see the modern Nomad Arab, the Arab is decidedly colored. The Roman officer took Paul for an Egyptian, Acts 21: 38-40 "Art not thou that Egyptian, which before these days maddest an uproar, and leddest out into the wilderness four thousand men that were murderers? But Paul said, I am a man which am a Jew of Tarsus, a city in Cilicia, a citizen of no mean city; and I beseech thee permit me to speak unto the people." And when he had given him license, Paul stood on the stairs, and beckoned with the hand unto the people. And when there was made a great silence, he spake unto them in the Hebrew tongue.

The Egyptian, ancient and modern are people of color. "I am black but comely, O ye daughters of Jerusalem," said an ancient Jewish Biblical writer. King Solomon, the writer of the book of proverbs, also the book of the Song of King Solomon 1:5-6. Huntington, in the character of races, says that the European and consequently the American is made up of three strains; the Negroid, Mediterranean and Caucasian. The cold winters have bleached out the Negroid color, but these strains have left its traces in the curly hair. Let me hasten to say that my mother had natural beautiful long straight hair in which I'm proud of. Whether this statement of Huntington is true or not, we may be certain that the races are mixed beneficially so we may also be reasonably sure that Jesus was not white. Daniel 7:9. "I beheld till the thrones were cast down, and the Ancient of days God, the eternal Father, whose garment was white as snow and the hair of his head like pure wool, his throne was like the fiery flame; and his wheels as burning fire." Yet many hold to what virtually amounts to the Religion of being white. It certainly is not the *Christian Christ Jesus of God's sacred Holy Word, The Bible.* The church has fearlessly and uncompromisingly taken its stand against race snobbery. Unless it does it cannot lead in a world where the superstition of blood will surely fade and the fact of character take its place for Fear of white prestige supremacy. This supremacy should not be the vocal point of our sight, nor our thoughts, what really should matter is that we comprehend and grasp in our mind, and understand the importance of receiving the Message, the word of God, for if we focus our attention on the outer appearance of the Messenger, *Christ Jesus the Messiah, whom God the Father sent the Creator,* the message will be somewhat lost. WE must not think as we have been taught in this world, that is to look at one another from our outer appearance, but listen from within our hearts and mind, and not by sight. "The Lord said to Samuel Look not on his appearance or at the height of his stature, for I have rejected him. For the Lord sees not as man sees; for man looks on the outward appearance, but the Lord looks on the Heart." 1 Samuel 16:7. As we are behind the closed doors of race exclusiveness, so we are behind the closed doors of national isolation for fear of being called unpatriotic. We have the feeling that *"Above all Nations is Humanity"* that narrow patriotism are being international uneasiness, that it is spirit that blocks disarmament, that fans trivial sparks into national flames and international configuration. We know that this isn't the thing that is confusing the world situation today, we know this, and yet we haven't the moral courage to speak out against it lest we be accused of committing the modern unpardonable sin-being unpatriotic. The world situation is crying to high heaven for someone to lead out of the narrow vicious circle in which we have become entangled to a human brotherhood and the church could do it but it is afraid of being called unpatriotic, and shuts the doors. The church is behind closed doors of mere routine of ritual for fear of breakdown. The early church was spontaneous; no one knew what it was going to do next. Now you can anticipate what the church will do. It is in ruts, a grave with both ends knocked out, "but ruts are so safe: when life ceases to be spontaneous we groove it in order to be sure we have something. We do have something, but whether it is life is the question.

On my many scenic trips across the country from the east coast to the west coast I was struck by the growing grandeur of the houses of worship and the increasing ornateness of ritual and liturgy. The feeling seems to be that the millennium lay just on the other side of an elaborate new church building, a vested choir, and stately processions. If life lay along this line, then Roman Catholicism would have it, for it makes Protestantism seem amateurish in this realm. Europe is filled with stately cathedrals and stale Christianity, with religious processions that is lost of movement. No, this is not the way to life; and yet filling the emptiness within, we add to the outer, hoping that the appearance of life will make life appear. History says it does not, nevertheless, we close our doors behind *safe* ritual for fear of break down and with fear of public opinion, very few people can be happy unless on the whole their way of life and their outlook and views on the world is approved by those with whom they have social relations and especially by those with whom they socialize and live. It is a distinctively characteristic, of modern communities that they are divided into sets which differ in their morals and their *Beliefs*.

* * *

PART SIX

WHY JESUS THE MESSIAH

"For the son of man is come to seek and to save that which was lost"

Luke 19:10

THE ANNUNCIATION BIRTH OF JESUS

Now in the sixth month there was sent on a mission from God the angel Gabriel to a city of Galilee named Nazareth, to a virgin promised in marriage to a man named Joseph, of the house of David. And the name of the virgin was Mary. And having come to her, she said, Be rejoicing because you have been encompassed with favor. The Lord is with you. But she was greatly agitated by reason of the word, and began reasoning what sort of an exotic greeting this might be. And the angel said to her, stop fearing, Mary, for you found favor in the presence of God. And behold: you shall conceive in your womb and you shall give birth to a son, and you shall call His name Jesus. This One shall be great, and Son of the. Most high shall He be called, and God, the Lord, shall give to Him the throne of David His father, and He shall reign as King over the house of Jacob forever and of His Kingdom there shall not be an end.

But Mary said to the angel, how shall this be possible, since I do not have an experiential knowledge of a man And the angel answering said to her, The holy spirit shall come upon you, and the power of the most high shall overshadow you. Wherefore also the holy thing which is being begotten shall be called son of God. And behold, Elizabeth, your Kinswoman also herself conceived a son in her old age, and this is the sixth month with her who is called sterile, for in the presence of God no word shall be impossible. And Mary said, Behold, the Lord's bondslave May it happen to me according to your word.

And the angel departed from her.

Luke 1:26-38

CONVERSION, A SPIRITUAL CHANGE IN HEART, AND BELIEF

And Jesus entered and passed through Jericho.

And behold, there was a man called by the name of Zacchaeus, And he himself was the collector of internal revenue for the district, having other tax collectors under his supervision. And he himself was wealthy. And he was endeavoring to see who Jesus was. And he was not able to do so because of the crowd, for he was small as to stature. And having run on ahead, he went up into a sycamore tree in order that he might see Him, because He was about to pass through that way. And as He came to the place Jesus having looked up, said to him, Zacchaeus, hurry, come down at once, for today at your home it is a necessity in the nature of the case for me to be a guest. And he came down in a hurry and welcomed Him as his guest, rejoicing. And having seen this, they all went to grumbling in undertone mutterings with one another, discontentedly complaining, saying that He had gone into be the house-guest of a man who was a notorious sinner. And Zacchaeus, having come to a standstill, said to the Lord, Behold, half of my possessions, Lord I now give at once to the poor. And since I have wrongfully cheated from individuals, I now restore at once four times as much. Jesus said to him, Today salvation came to this home, because he himself is also a son of Abraham,

For the son of man came to seek and to save that which has been lost.

Luke 19:1-10"

FROM DARKNESS TO LIGHT, UNTO GOD

For a period of time men were lost in spiritual darkness, blinded by sin, searching, questing, seeking some way out. Man needed someone who could lead him out of the mental confusion, someone who could redeem him from the Devil's prison, someone who could unlock the prison doors. Men with hungry hearts, thirsty minds, and broken spirits stood hopelessly with searching eyes and listening ears. Meanwhile the Devil gloated over his mighty victory in the Garden of Eden.

From the primitive man in the jungle through the mighty civilizations of Egypt, Greece, and Rome, bewildered men were all asking the same question, "How can I get out? How can I be better? What can I do? Which way can I turn? How can I get rid of this terrible blindness. How can I stop this overpowering torrent? How can I get out of the mesh in which I find myself? If there is a way, how can I find it?"

We have already seen that the Bible teaches that God was a God of love. He wanted to do something for man. He wanted to save man. He wanted to free man from the curse of sin. How could He do it? God was a just God. He was righteous, and holy. He had warned man from the beginning that if he obeyed the Devil and disobeyed God, he would die physically and spiritually. Man deliberately disobeyed God. Man had to die or God would have been a liar, for God could not break His word. His very nature would not allow Him to lie. His word had to be kept. Therefore, when man deliberately disobeyed Him, he was banished from the presence of God. He deliberately chose to go the Devil's way. God could not freely forgive man's sin, or God would have found Himself in the impossible position of lying, because HE HAD SAID, "in the day that thou eatest thereof, thou shalt surely die"

There had to be some other way, for man was helplessly lost and hopelessly involved. Man's very nature was helplessly lost and hopelessly involved. Man's very nature was inverted. He opposed God. Many even denied that God existed, so blinded were they by the disease of sin from which they suffered. Proverbs 20:-9 But even in the garden of Eden, God gave a hint that He was going to do something about it. He wanted the Devil and promised man, "And I will put enmity between thee and the woman, and between thy seed and her seed; it shall bruise thy head, and thou shalt bruise his heel." and thou shalt bruise his heel"-here was a brilliant flash of light from heaven. Here was a promise. Here was something that man could hold on to. God was promising that someday a redeemer would come, a DELIVERER would come. God gave man hope. Down through the centuries man held on to that one bit of hope!

That was not all. There were other occasions through the thousands of years of history when other flashes of light came from heaven. All through the Old Testament, God gave man the promise of salvation if by faith he would believe in the coming redeemer. Therefore God began to teach His people that man could only be saved by substitution. Someone else would have to pay the bill for mans' redemption.

Go back again with me in your imagination to Eden for a moment God said, "In the day that thou eatest thereof thou shalt surely die, "Man did eat of it. He died.

Suppose that God had said, "Adam, you must have made a mistake that was a slight error on your part. You are forgiven. Please don't do it again." God would have been a liar. He would not have been holy, neither would He have been just. He was forced by His very nature to keep His word. God's justice was at stake. Man had to die spiritually and physically. His iniquities (the practice of evil immoral sin.) Disobedience separated him from his god. Thus man had to suffer. He had to pay for his own sins. As we have seen, Adam was the federal head of the human race. When Adam sinned, we all sinned.

"Wherefore, as by one man sin entered into the world, and death by sin; and so death passed upon all men, for that all have sinned." Romans 5:12

The burning question became "How can God be just and still justify the sinner?" It must be remembered that the word justify means the "clearance of the soul from guilt." Justification is far more than just forgiveness. Sin must be put away and made as though it had never been. Man must be restored so that there shall be no spot or blemish or stain. In other words, man must be taken back to the position he had before he fell from grace.

For centuries men in their blindness have been trying to get back to Eden-but they have never been able to reach their goal. They have tried many paths, but they have all failed. Education is necessary, but education will not bring a man back to God. False religions are an opiate which keep men from present misery while on their way to future glory, but they will never bring man to the place of his goal. The

United Nations may be a practical necessity in a world of men of war, and we are thankful for every step that can be taken in the field of international relations that can settle disputes without recourse to war; but if the United Nations could bring lasting peace, man could say to God, "We do not need You anymore. We have brought peace on earth and have organized humanity in righteousness." All of these schemes are patchwork remedies that the world must use while waiting for the Great Physician. Back in history we know that the first attempt of united man ended with the confusion of tongues at the Tower of Babel

Men have failed on every other occasion when they have tried to work without God, and they must be doomed to such failures.

The question remains "how can god be just-that is, true to Himself in nature and true to Himself in holiness, and yet justify the sinner?" Because each man had to bear his own sins, all mankind was excluded from helping, since each was contaminated with the same sins.

The only solution was for an innocent party to volunteer to die physically and spiritually as a substitution before God. This innocent party would have to take man's judgment, penalty, and death But where was such an individual? Certainly there was none on earth, for the Bible says, "all have sinned." There was only one possibility. God's own son was the only personality in the universe who had the capacity to bear in His own body the sins of the World.

Certainly Gabriel might possibly have come and died for one person, but only God's Son was infinite and thus able to die for all The Bible teaches that God is actually three Persons. This is a mystery that we will never be able to understand. The Bible does not teach that there are three Gods-but that there is one God. This one God, however, is expressed in three Persons. There is God the Father, God the

Son, and God the Spirit. The Second Person of this Godhead is God's Son, Jesus Christ. He is co-equal with God the Father. He was not a Son of God but the Son of God. He is the Eternal Son of God-the Second person of the Godhead, God manifested in the flesh, the living savior. The Bible teaches that Jesus Christ had no beginning. He was never created. The Bible teaches that the heavens were created by Him. All the myriads of stars and flaming suns were created by Hi m. The earth was flung from His flaming finger tip. The birth of Jesus Christ that we celebrate at Christmas time was not His beginning. His origin is shrouded in that same mystery that baffles u s when we inquire into the beginning of God. The Bible only tells us, "in the beginning was the word, and the word was with God and the word was God" The Bible teaches us, that in the sixth day the creation of man) (described in Genesis J:26 And God said, Let us make man in our image, after our likeness:

The Bible teaches us, "Who is the image of the invisible God, the first born of every creature: For by Him were all things created, that are in heaven, and that are in earth, visible and invisible, whether they be thrones, or dominions, or principalities, or powers: all things were created by Him, and for Him: And He is before all things, and by Him all things consist.

That last phrase indicates that He holds all things together. In other words the entire universe would smash into billions of atoms was it not for the cohesive power of Jesus Christ. The Bible again says, And, Thou, Lord, in the beginning hast laid the foundation of the earth, and the heavens are the works of Thine hands: They shall perish; but Thou remainest; and they all shall wax old as doth a garment; and as a vesture shalt Thou fold them up, and they shall be changed: but Thou art the same, and Thy years shall not fail.."

Again Jesus said of Himself, "I am Alpha and Omega, the beginning and the end," He, and HE alone, had the power and capacity to bring man back to God. But would He? If He did, He would have to come to earth. He would have to take the form of a servant. He would have to be made in the likeness of men. He would have to humble Himself and become obedient unto death. He would have to grapple with sin. He would have to meet and overcome Satan, the enemy of man's soul. He would have to buy sinners out of the slave market of sin. He would have to lose the bonds

and set the prisoners free by paying a price-that price would be His own blood. He would have to be despised and rejected of men, a man of sorrows and acquainted with grief. He would have to be smitten of God and separated from God. He would have to be wounded for the transgressions of men and bruised for their iniquities. (the practice of evil immoral sin)The Bible teaches us in 2 Timothy 2:18-19 "Who concerning the truth have erred, saying that the Resurrection is past already, and overthrow the faith of some never-the-less the foundation of God standeth sure having this seal, the Lord Knoweth them that are his, and let everyone that nameth the name of Christ depart from iniquity."

He would have to reconcile God and man. He would be the great mediator of history. He would have to be a substitute. He would have to die in the place of sinful man. All this would have to be done, voluntarily.

Thanks be unto God-that is exactly what happened! Looking down over the battlements of heaven He saw this planet swinging in space-doomed, damned, crushed, and bound for hell. He saw you and me struggling beneath our load of sin and bound in the chains and ropes of sin. He made His decision in the council halls of God. The angelic hosts bowed in humility and awe as heaven's Prince of Peace and Lord of Lords, who could speak worlds into space, got into His jeweled chariot, went through pearly gates, across the steep of the skies, and on a black Judean night, while the stars sang together and the escorting angels chanted His praises, stepped out of the chariot, threw off His robes, and became man!

It was as though I, was walking along a road, stepped on an ant-hill. I might look down and say to the ants, "I am terribly sorry that I've stepped on your ant-hill. I've disrupted your home. Everything is in confusion. I wish I could tell you that I loved you, that I did not mean to do it, that I would like to help you.

But you say, 'That's absurd, that's impossible, ants cannot understand your language!' That's just it! How wonderful it would be if I could only become an ant for a few moments and in their own language tell them of my love for them!

That, in effect, is what Christ did. He came to reveal God to men. He it is who told us that God loves us and is interested in our lives. He it is who told us of the mercy and long-suffering and grace of God. He it is who promised life everlasting.

But more than that, Jesus Christ partook of flesh and blood in order that He might die. He was manifested to take away our sins. Christ came into this world to give His life a ransom for many. The very purpose of Christ's coming into the world was that he might offer up his life as a sacrifice for the sins of men. He came to die. The shadow of His death hung like a pall over all of His thirty-three years.

The night Jesus was born Satan trembled. He sought to slay Him before He was born, and tried to slay Him as soon as He was born when the decree went forth from Herod ordering the slaughter of all the children, its one purpose was to make certain of the death of Jesus.

All the days of His life on earth He never once committed a sin; He is the only man who ever lived that was sinless. He could stand in front of men and say, "Which of you convinceth me of sin? He was hounded by the enemy day and night, but they never found any sin in Him. He was without spot or blemish.

Jesus lived a humble life. He made Himself of no reputation. He received no honor of men. He was born in a stable. He was reared in the insignificant village of Nazareth. He was a carpenter He gathered around Him a humble group of fishermen as His followers. He walked among men as a man. He put on no superior air and sought no worldly preferment. He humbled Himself as no other man has ever humbled himself.

Jesus taught with such authority that the people of His day said, "Never man spake like this man." Every word that He spoke was historically true. Every word that He spoke was scientifically true. Every word that He spoke was ethically true. There were no loopholes in the moral conceptions and statements of Jesus Christ His ethical vision was wholly correct, correct in the age in which He lived and correct in every age that has followed it.

The words of this blessed Person were prophetically true. He prophesied many things that are even yet in the future. Lawyers tried to catch Him with test questions, but they could never confuse Him His answers to His opponents were clear and clean-cut. There were no questions marks about His statements, no vagueness in His meaning, no hesitancy in His words. He knew, and therefore spoke with quit authority. He spoke with such simplicity that the common people heard Him gladly. Though His words were profound, yet they were plain. His words were weighty, but easily understood. They shone with a luster and simplicity of statement that staggered His enemies. He dealt with the great questions of the day in such a way that a wayfaring man had no difficulty in following Him.

The Lord Jesus cured the sick, the lame, and the blind healed the leper and raised the dead. He cast out demons. He quieted the elements. He stilled the storms. He brought peace, joy and hope to the thousands to whom He ministered.

He showed no sign of fear. He was never in a hurry. He met with no accidents. He moved with perfect co-ordination and precision. He had supreme poise of bearing. He did not waver or worry about His work.

He stood before Pilate and quietly said, "Thou couldst have no power at all against me, except it were given thee from above." He told the frightened people that angelic legions were at His command.

He approached His cross with dignity and calmness, with an assurance and a set purpose that fulfilled the prophecy written about Him eight hundred years earlier: "He is brought as a lamb to the slaughter, and as a sheep before her shearers is dumb, so He open not His mouth."

1 j He moved supremely, gloriously, and with great anticipation toward the mission that He had come to accomplish. He had come to save sinful men. He had come to appease the wrath of God. He had come to buy men from the slave market of the Devil. He had come to defeat the devil forever. He had come to conquer hell and the grave. There was only one way that He could do it. There was only one course set before Him.

His death had been prophesied thousands of years before. First, as we have seen, in Eden's Garden; and then in sermon, story, and prophecy the death of Christ was set forth in the ages past. Abraham foresaw His death as the lamb was slain. The children of Israel symbolized His death in the slaughtered lamb Every time blood was shed on a Jewish altar it represented the Lamb of God who was someday to come and take away sin. David prophesied His death in more than one prophetic Psalm. Isaiah gave whole chapters to predicting the details of His death.

Jesus Christ said that He had power to lay down His life when He said, "The good shepherd giveth his life for the sheep." He said again, 'Even so must the Son of man be lifted up: That whosoever believeth in him should not perish." Jesus Christ had face d the possibility of the cross far back in eternity. During all the ages which preceded His birth, He knew that the day of His death was hastening on. When He was born of a virgin, He was born with the cross darkening His pathway. He had taken on a human body in order that He might die. From the cradle to the cross, His purpose was to die. He suffered as no man has ever suffered: "The night watches in Gethsemane, lighted by the flaming torches, Kiss of the traitor, the arrest, the trial before the high priest, the hour of waiting, the palace of the Roman governor, the journey to the palace of Herod,

the rough handling by Herod's brutal soldiers, the awesome scenes while Pilate tried to save Him as priests and people clamored for His blood, the scourging, the howling multitudes, the path from Jerusalem to Golgotha, the nails in His hands, the spike through His feet, the crowd of thorns upon His brow, the sarcastic and mocking cries of the two thieves on either side, 'You have saved others, now save yourself,"

Sometimes people have asked me why Christ died so quickly, in six hours, on the cross, while other victims have agonized on the cross for two and three days. He was weak and exhausted when He came there. He had been scourged, He was physically depleted. But when Christ died, h e died voluntarily. He chose the exact moment when He expired.

There He hung naked between heaven and earth. They had pulled His beard until His face bled. They had spat in His face until His face was running with the spittle of angry men. He voiced neither complaint nor appeal but simply a statement by which He let us know in two words something of the terrible physical pain He suffered when He said, "I thirst" The blood was being extracted. God demands death, either for the sinner or a substitute. Christ was the substitute! Gabriel and ten legions of angels hovered on the rim of the universe, their swords unsheathed. One look from His blessed face and they would have swept the angry, shouting multitudes into hell. The spikes never held Him-it was the cords of love that bound tighter than any nails that men could mold. "But God commendeth His love toward us, in that, while we were yet sinners, Christ died for us."

For you! For me! He bore our sins in His body upon the tree. As someone has said, "Behold Him on the Cross, bending His sacred head, and gathering into His heart in the awful isolation of separation from God the issue of the sin of the world, and see how out of that acceptance of the issue of sin He creates that which He does not require for Himself that He may distribute to those whose place He has taken. "Standing overwhelmed in the presence of this suffering, feeling our own inability to understand or explain, and with a great sense of might and majesty overwhelming us we hear the next words that pass His lips, "It is finished".

But the physical suffering of Jesus Christ was not the real suffering. Many men before Him had died. Many men had become martyrs The awful suffering of Jesus Christ was His spiritual death. He reached the final issue of sin, fathomed the deepest sorrow, when God turned His back and hid His face so that He cried, "My God, why hast Thou forsaken me?" Alone in the supreme hour of mankind1 s history Christ uttered these words! Light blazed forth to give us a glimpse of what He was enduring, but the light was so blinding,

He who knew no sin was made to be sin on our behalf that we might become the righteousness of god in him. On the cross He was made sin. He was God-forsaken. Because he knew no sin there is a value beyond comprehension in the penalty He bore, a penalty that He did not need for Himself. If in bearing sin in His own body He created a value that He did not need for Himself, for whom was the value created?

How it was accomplished in the depth of the darkness man will never know. I know only one thing-he bore my sins in His body upon the tree. He stood where I should have stood. The pain of hell that were my portion were heaped on Him, and I am able to go to heaven and merit that which is not my own, but is His by right. All types, the offerings, the shadows, and the symbols of the Old Testament were now fulfilled. No longer do the priests have to enter once a year into the Holiest place.

The sacrifice was penal, substitutionary, redemptive, propitiatory, reconciliatory, efficacious, and as it is appointed unto men once to die, but after this the judgment, so Christ was once offered to bear the sins of many."

Now that the ground of redemption has been laid, all the guilty sinner has to do is "believe on the son" And have Peace with God. "For god so loved the world, that he gave his only begotten son, that whosoever believeth in him should not perish, but have everlasting life."

'For God sent not his son into the world to condemn the world: but that the world through him might be saved!' John 3:16-17

In the cross of Christ I see three things: First, a description of the depth of man's sin. Do not blame the people of that day for putting Christ to the cross. You and I are just as guilty. It w as not the people or the Roman soldiers that put him to the cross it was my sins and your sins that made it necessary for Him to volunteer this death.

Second, in the cross I see the overwhelming "love   of God". If ever we should doubt the love of God, take a long, deep look at the cross, for in the cross you find the "expression of God's love".

Third, in the cross is the only "way of salvation." Jesus said, "I am the way, the truth and the life: no man cometh unto the father but by Me."

If ye had known me, ye should have known my Father also: and From henceforth ye know him, and have seen him. John 14:6-7

There is no possibility of being saved from sin and hell, except by identifying yourself with the Christ of the cross. If there had been any other way to save us, He would have found it.

If reformation, or living a good moral and ethical life would have saved us, Jesus never would have died.

NOTHING CAN BE ADDED
TO COMPLETENESS

The Bible teaches us, in Colossians 2:8-10 "Beware lest any spoil you through philosophy and vain deceit, after the tradition of men, after the rudiments of the world, and not after Christ. For in him dwelleth all the fullness of the Godhead bodily. And ye are complete in him, which is the head of all principality and powers." A substitute had to take our place. Men do not like to talk about it. They do not like to hear about it because of being exposed, of our sinful nature, They do not like to hear about it because it injures our pride. It takes all self out.

Many people say, "Can i not be saved by living by the golden rule? Or following the precepts of Jesus? Or living the ethical 1ife that Jesus taught?" Even if we could be saved by living the life that Jesus taught, we still would be a sinner. We still would fail, because none of us have ever lived the life that Jesus taught from the time we were born till the time we die. We have failed. We have transgressed. We have disobeyed. We have sinned. Therefore, what are we going to do about our sins? There is only one thing to do and that is to bring it to the cross and find forgiveness.

Years ago King Charles V was loaned a large sum of money by a merchant in Antwerp. The note came due, but the King was bankrupt and unable to pay. The merchant gave a great banquet for the King. When all the guest were seated and before the food was brought in, the merchant had a large platter placed on the table before him and a fire lighted on it. Then, taking the note out of his pocket, he held it in the flame until it was burned to ashes The King threw his arm around his benefactor and wept.

Just so, we have all been morgaged to God. The debt was due, but we were unable to pay. Two thousand years ago God invited the world to the gospel feast, and in the agonies of the cross, God held our sins until every last vestige of our guilt was consumed.

The Bible says, "Without shedding of blood is no remission. Many people have said to me, "How repulsive! You don't mean to tell us that you believe in a slaughterhouse religion" Others have wondered, "I do not understand why God demands blood" Many people have wondered, "I cannot understand why Christ had to die for me. "Today the idea of the shed blood of Christ is becoming old-fashioned and out of date in a lot of preaching, but it is still there. It is in the bible. It is the very heart of Christianity. The distinctive feature of Christianity is blood atonement. Without it we cannot be saved. Blood is actually a symbol of the death of Christ.

The Bible teaches that it first of all redeems. "Forasmuch as y e know that ye were not redeemed with corruptible things, as silver and gold, from our vain conversation received by tradition from your fathers: But with the precious blood of Christ, as of a lamb without blemish and without spot." Not only are we redeemed from the hands of the Devil, but from the hands of the law. Christ's death on the cross brings us out from under the law. The law condemned us, but Christ satisfied every claim. All the gold and silver and the precious stones of earth could never have bought us. What they could not do, the death of Christ did Redemption means "buying back." We had been sold for nothing to the Devil, but Christ redeemed us and brought us back.

Second it brings us nigh. "But now in Christ Jesus ye who sometimes were far off are made nigh by the blood of Christ. When we were "aliens from the common wealth of Israel, and strangers from the covenants of promise, having no hope, and without God in the world," Jesus Christ brought us nigh unto God. "There is therefore now no judgment to them which are in Christ Jesus." The redeemed sinner will never have to face the judgment of "Almighty God. Christ has already taken his judgment.

Third, it makes peace. "And having made peace through the blood of his cross, by Him to reconcile all things unto Himself; by Him, I say, whether they be things in earth, or things in heaven.

The world will never know peace until it finds it in the cross of Jesus Christ. We will never know the peace with god, peace of conscience, peace of mind, and peace of soul, until we stand at the foot of the cross and. Identify yourself with Christ by faith. There is the secret of peace. This is peace with god.

Fourth, it justifies. "Much more then, being now justified by his blood, we shall be saved from wrath through Him. It changes men's standing before God. It is a change from guilt and condemnation to pardon and forgiveness. The forgiven sinner is not like the discharged prisoner who has served out his term and is discharged but with no further rights of citizenship. The repentant sinner, is pardoned through the blood of Jesus Christ, regains his full citizenship. "Who shall lay anything to the charge of God's elect? It is God that justifieth. Who is he that condemneth? It is Christ that died, yea rather, that is risen again, who is even at the right hand of God, who also maketh intercession for us."

Fifth, it cleanses. "But if we walk in the light, as He is in the light, we have fellowship one with another, and the blood of Jesus Christ his son cleanseth us from all sin." First John 1:7, The Key word in this verse is all. Not part of our sins but all of them. Every lie we ever told, every mean, low-down dirty thing that we ever did, our hypocrisy, our lustful thoughts-all are cleansed by the death of Christ.

The story has often been told that years ago, in London, there was a large gathering of noted people, and among the invited guests was a famous preacher of his day, Caesar Milan. A young lady played and sang charmingly and everyone was delighted. Very graciously, tactful, and yet boldly the preacher went up to her after the music had ceased and said, "I thought as I listened to you tonight, how tremendously the cause of Christ would be benefited if your talents were dedicated to His cause. You know, young lady you are as much a sinner in the sight of God as a drunkard in the ditch or a harlot on the street. But I'm glad to tell you that the blood of Jesus Christ, His Son, can cleanse from all sin."

The young woman snapped out a rebuke for his presumption, to which he replied, "Lady, I mean no offense. I pray God's spirit will convict you."

They all returned to their homes. The young woman retired but could not sleep. The face of the preacher appeared before her and his words rang through her mind. At two o'clock in the morning she sprang from her bed, took a pencil and paper, and with tears dripping from her face, Charlotte Elliott wrote that famous poem:

Just as I am, without one plea, But that Thy blood was shed for me, And that Thou bidd'st me come to Thee, Olamb of God, I come I come!

Just as I am and waiting not to rid my soul of one dark blot, To Thee, whose blood can cleanse each spot, Olamb of God, I come I come.

But this is not the end. We do not leave Christ hanging on a cross with blood streaming down from His hands, His side, and His feet. He is taken down and laid carefully away in a tomb. A big stone is rolled against the entrance of the tomb, soldiers are set to guard it. All day Saturday, His followers sit gloomily and s sadly in the upper room. Two have already started toward Emmaus. Fear has gripped them all. Early on that first Easter morning, Mary, Mary Magdalene, and Salome make their way to the tomb to anoint the dead body. When they arrive, they are startled to find the tomb is empty. An angel is standing at the head of the tomb and asks, "Whom do you seek?" And they reply, "We seek Jesus of Nazareth." And then the angel gives the greatest, most glorious news that human ear has ever heard, "He is not here. He is risen!! Mark- 16: 1 -20- (6)

THE PROMISE

Upon that great fact hangs the entire plan of the redemptive program of God. Without the resurrection there could be no salvation. Christ predicted His resurrection many times. He said on one occasion, "For as Jonah was three days and three nights in the whale's belly; so shall the Son of man be three days and three nights in the heart of the earth." As He predicted, He rose!

There are certain laws of evidence which hold in the establishment of any historic event. There must be documentation of the event in question made by reliable contemporary witnesses. There is more evidence that Jesus rose from the dead than there is that Julius Caesar ever lived or that Alexander the Great died at the age of thirty three. It is strange that historians will accept thousands of facts for which they can produce only shreds of evidence. But in the face of the overwhelming evidence of the resurrection of Jesus Christ they cast a skeptical eye and hold intellectual doubts. The trouble with these people is that they do not want to believe. Their spiritual vision is so blinded and they are so completely prejudiced that they cannot accept the glorious fact of the resurrection of Christ on Bible testimony alone.

The resurrection meant, first, that Christ was God of very God. He was what He claimed to be. Christ was Deity in the flesh.

Second, it meant that God had accepted His atoning work on the cross of Christ, which was necessary to our salvation. "Who was delivered for our offence, and was raised again for our justification."

Third, it assures mankind of a righteous judgment. Fourth, it guarantees that our bodies also will be raised in the end. "But now is Christ risen from the dead, and became the first fruit of them that slept." The Scripture teaches that as Christians, our bodies may go to the grave but they are going to be raised on the great resurrection morning. Then will death be swallowed up in victory. As a result of the resurrection of Christ the sting of death is gone and Christ has the keys of death. He says, "I am He that liveth, and was dead; and, behold, I am alive forevermore, Amen; and have the key of hell and of death." And Christ promises that "because I live, ye shall live also." John 14:15-21-19.And, fifth, it means that death is abolished. The power of death has been broken and death's fear has been removed.

Spiritual obedience is most needful for a Christian today,. Ignore therefore, the groundless suspicion that we sin by obeying and walk confident in this path exempt us from danger.

"We sometimes fear" I that in obeying God we act against the dictates of our conscience, whereas, on the contrary, we really increase our merit before God.

Now we can say with the Psalmist, "Yea, though I walk through the valley of the shadow of death, I will fear no evil; for Thou art with me; Thy rod and Thy staff they comfort me."Psalm 23:1

Paul looked forward to death with great anticipation as a result of the resurrection of Christ. He said, "For to me to live is Christ, and to die is gain."

Without the resurrection of Christ there could be no hope for the future. The Bible promises that someday we are going to stand face to face with the resurrected Christ, and we are going to have bodies like unto His own body.

FACE TO FACE WITH CHRIST JESUS THE MESSIAH.

PART SEVEN

REFORMATION

"Beware lest any spoil you through philosophy and vain deceit, after the tradition of men, after the rudiments of the world, and not after Christ. For in him dwelleth all the fullness of the Godhead bodily. And ye are complete in him, which is the head of all principality and power."

Colossians 2:8-10

This state of affairs began with the Reformation, the beginning of the Protestant Churches, in a great religious movement in the 16th century in hope of making over for the better, to make better by removing *faults and flaws*, by a *change* in one's *character*. Perhaps one should say with the Renaissance, and has grown more and more ever since. There were Protestants and Catholics, who differed not only in theology but on many more practical matters. There were aristocrats who permitted various kinds of action that were not tolerated among the bourgeoisie.

Then there came to be liberal beliefs and opinions, and free thinkers, who did not recognize the duties of religious observance. In our own day through out the mainland of Europe, one of the six greatest division of the Earths land surface, there is a profound division between socialists and others not only politics but almost every department of life. In English speaking countries the division are very numerous. In some sets devotion to the Empire is the supreme virtue, in others it is considered a vice, and in others a form of stupidity. Conventional people consider adultery one of the worse of crimes, but large sections of the population regard it as *Excusable.* Among Catholics divorce is suppose to be totally forbidden, while most non-Catholics accept it as a necessary alleviation of matrimony. Owing to all these differences of outlook a person of given tastes and convictions may find himself practically an outcast while he lives in one set, although in another set he would be accepted as an entirely ordinary human being. *Yet the Holy Bible in which we are suppose to be living by says differ (Matthew 5:31-32) The word of the "Lord" says, it has also been said, "Whoever divorces his wife must give her a certificate of divorce."* But I tell you, whoever dismisses and repudiates refuse to recognize, and divorces his wife, except on the grounds of unfaithfulness, (sexual immorality), causes her to commit adultery, and whoever marries a woman who has been divorced commits adultery." (Deuteronomy 24:1-4. "Thus said the *Lord God.* When a man takes a wife and marries her, if then she finds no favor in his eyes because he has found some indecency in her, and he writes her a bill of divorce, puts it in her hand, and sends her out of his house she goes and marries another man, and if the latter husband dislikes her and writes her a bill of divorce and puts it in her hand and send her out of his house, or if the latter husband dies, Who took her as his wife, the other former husband, who sent her away, may not take her again to be his wife after she is defiled. For that is an abomination before the Lord."

A very great deal of unhappiness among the young arises in this way. A young man or young woman some how catches ideas that are in the air, but finds that these ideas are considered a curse, in the particular environment in which he or she lives. It seems to the young as if the only environment which they are acquainted were representative of the whole world. They can scarcely believe that in another place or another set the views which they dare not avow for fear of being thought utterly perverse would be accepted as the ordinary common place of the age.

Thus through ignorance of the world a great deal of unnecessary misery is endured, sometimes only in youth, but not infrequently through out life. This isolation is not only a source of pain; it also causes a great dissipation of energy in the unnecessary task of maintaining mental independence against hostile *surrounding*, but there are not many who have this degree of force in their inner life. To almost everybody are sympathetic surroundings are necessary to happiness. To the majority of course, the surroundings in which they happen to find themselves are pathetic. They take in as to imbibe knowledge of prejudices in youth, and instinctively adapt themselves to the beliefs and customs which they find in existence around them. But to a large minority, which includes practically all who have any intellectual or artistic merit, this attitude of as an accepted fact or condition is impossible. A person born, let us say, in some small country town finds himself from early youth surrounded by hostility to everything that is necessary for mental excellence. If he wishes to read serious books, other boys despise him and teachers tell him that such works are unsettling. If he cares for art, his contemporary people living at the same time think him unmanly and his elders think him immoral. If he desires any career, however respectable, which has not been common in the circle to which he belongs, he is told that he is setting himself up, and that what was good enough for his father ought to be good enough for him. If he shows any tendency to criticize his parents, religious beliefs or political affiliations he is likely to find himself in serious trouble. For all these reasons to most young men an young women of exceptional merit adolescence is a time of great unhappiness. To their more ordinary companions it may be a time of gayety and enjoyment, but for themselves they want something more serious, which they can't find neither among their elders nor among their contemporaries in the particular social setting in which chance has caused them to be born. When such young people go to a university they probably discover having similar tastes, ideas, and ideals suitable to ones need and years of great happiness. If they are fortunate, they may succeed on leaving the university, in obtaining some kind of work that gives them still the possibility of choosing similar and suitable companions.

This is especially true in America, because of the great boundaries of the country. In the most unlikely places, north, south, east, and west, one finds lonely individuals who know from books that there are places where they would not be lonely, but who have no chance to live in such places, and only the rarest opportunity of a similar and suitable conversation. Where public opinion is always more overbearing and cruel, towards those who obviously fear it than towards those who feel indifferent to it, a dog will bark more loudly and bite more readily when people are afraid of him than when they treat him with contempt, and the human herd has something of this same characteristic. If you show that you are afraid of them, you give promise of good hunting, whereas if you show indifference, they begin to doubt their own power and therefore tend to let you alone.

I am not of course thinking of extreme forms of challenging, or resisting. If we hold in California the views that are conventional in Russia, or in Russia the views that are conventional in California, you must accept the consequences. I am thinking, not of such extremes, but of much milder lapse from following common customs and formalities, such as failure to dress correctly or to belong to some church or to abstain from reading intelligent books. This is largely a matter of a certain kind of good nature and friendliness. Conventional people are roused to fury by departures from convention, largely because they regard such departures as a criticism of themselves. They will pardon much unconventionality in a man who has enough encouragement and friendliness to make it clear, even to the stupidest, that he is not engaged in critical them. This method of escaping harsh criticism is, however, impossible to many of those whose tastes or opinions cause them to be out of sympathy with the group as a whole.

This lack of sympathy makes them uncomfortable and causes them to have a quarrelsome attitude, even if outwardly they conform or manage to avoid any sharp issue. People who are not in harmony with the fixed generally accepted followed customs of their own set end therefore to be causing a sting and uncomfortable and lacking in expansive good humor. These same people transported into another set, where their outlook is not thought strange, will seem to change their *character* entirely. From being serious, shy and retiring they may become *lively* and self-confident; from being conformed to a new environment, he may become smooth and easy; from being self-centered he may become sociable, and one whose interest is directed outward towards *external matters*. Where ever possible, therefore, young people who find themselves out of harmony with their surroundings should endeavor in the choice of a profession to select some career which will give them a chance of having suitable taste, ideas, environment and similar companionship, even if this should entail a considerable loss of income. Often they hardly know that this is possible, since their knowledge of the world is very limited, and they may easily imagine that the prejudices to which they have become accustomed to at *home* and *world-wide.*

(This is a matter which older men and women should have the desire to give assistance to the young, since a considerable experience of mankind is necessary in having essential joy.) Happiness and joy is promoted by associations of people with similar tastes and similar opinions. Social relations between individuals or groups may be expected to develop more and more along the lines, and it may be hoped that by these means the loneliness that now afflicts so many people will be gradually diminished almost to the vanishing point. This will undoubtedly increase their happiness, but it will of course diminish the sadistic pleasure which at present derive from having people at their mercy. I don't think, however, that this is a pleasure which we need be greatly concerned to preserve.

Fear of public opinion, like every other form of *fear*, is oppressive and *stunts growth*. It is difficult to achieve any kind of greatness while a fear of this kind remains strong, and it is impossible to acquire that freedom of spirit in which true happiness consist, for it is essential to happiness that our way of living should spring from our deep impulses and not from the accidental taste and desires of those who happen to be our neighbors, or even our relations. Fear of immediate neighbors is no doubt less than it was, but there is a new kind of fear, namely, the fear of what newspapers may say. This is quite as terrifying as anything connected with the middle age, medieval witch hunt. When the newspaper chooses to make a scapegoat of some perhaps quite harmless person the results may be very terrible. Fortunately, as yet this is a fate which most people escape through being without fame; but as publicity gets more and more perfect in its methods, there will be an increasing danger of social persecution. This is a matter to be viewed by individuals held in contempt who is the victim, and what ever maybe thought of the great principle of the freedom of the press. I think the line will have to be drawn more sharply than it is by the existing media and publications that is unjustly injurious to someone's reputation, (libel laws) and anything will have to be forbidden that makes life intolerable for innocent individuals, even if they should happen to have done or said things spiteful which can cause them to become unpopular. The only ultimate *cure* for this evil is, however, an increase of *toleration* on the part of the public. The best way to increase *toleration* is to multiply the number of individuals who enjoy real happiness and do not therefore find their chief pleasure in the infliction of pain upon their *fellowman*.

I believe *Reformation* can be obtain if we as individuals begin in hope, of making over for better by removing, *faults*, and *flaws*, by a *change* in our *character, behavior, and attitudes*, of the way we feel and think about one another. And I believe we can as a people, make this world a better place if we just *try*.

* * *

PART EIGHT

RESTORATION by MEANS
of RECONCILIATION

The act of harmonizing to restore to a state of harmony, in relations to adjust harmoniously, as to reconcile science and religion.

There are those who are always talking of free trade, but no one has yet succeeded in translating their ideas or ideals into reality. First, we must understand the world in which we live today. It is a complex world, very different from that which out grandparents knew only a few generations ago. We are amazed to find that within the past hundred years, almost within the memory of living men, the population of the world has more than doubled. More profound changes in population in the last two centuries than in the thousands of years of human history which went before. Science and invention have worked a revolution in the ways in which men live. They have transformed industry and agriculture travel and communication. Only a century ago many families in the most advanced nations raised their own food, wove their own clothing and built their own homes. Overnight the pioneer and colonial periods have passed overnight the population of the world has doubled; overnight modern science has given us the means of uniting or destroying the world. This new world of science is not as simple as the old one. It calls for new ways of thought and new methods of management. Men and nations are no longer independent parts of a complex whole. But because this revolution came so suddenly, there has not yet been time for men and nations to adjust themselves to the vast changes which have taken place. Some call this period in which we live an age of *"Transition"* one finds startling paradoxes absurd or incredible.

In a world where interdependence requires cooperation, honest sincerity, one still finds competition and conflict. In a world which is united by modern methods of transportation and communication, nations are straining every energy to build military and economic walls around themselves, to insulate themselves in air-tight compartments. In a world where there is the possibility of abundance, one finds poverty and suffering. The problem of peaceful change is a part of this modern paradox. In the years since the war the demand for change has become year by year more insistent. It has produced revolutions and profound upheavals within national boundaries, and was or the use of armed forces across national borders. These demands for change in the existing order of things arise from certain primary desires of men and nations. One is the desire for security, individual security against hunger and unemployment, national security against attack or foreign domination. Another is the desire for a decent standard of living.

But in consideration the cause of friction between nations, two other desires must also be taken into account. These are power and prestige. Governments are naturally concerned with improving the conditions of their people, but they are also very much concerned with gaining a position of power which will give them an advantage in their relations with other nations. And the important thing to note is that the desire for power, which originally was only a means to enable a country to carry out its policy, often becomes an end in itself. It may actually become a major objective of foreign policy. This is what is meant by the sinister term *"Power Politics"* which became so familiar in the nineteenth and twentieth centuries. *"Prestige,"* which usually means reputation for power has been sought by nations because it enables them to command Fear or Respect from others, and thus strengthens their influence in world politics. On the other hand, the demand for change in the *Status Quo may arise from conditions of actual need.* The government may be concerned with the vital matter of the living standard of its people; what they have to eat, what kind of clothing they wear, what sort of houses they live in, what chance they or their children have of being well educated, whether they have proper Medical Care, in other words whether they can enjoy the benefits of modern civilization. These are questions which every nation has a right to ask in an age when *Science and Technology* offers the possibility of an adequate living standard for all. Yet this possibility is far from being realized in overpopulated nations poor in natural resources and without sufficient land to support their people. The problem of peaceful change is not merrily how to remove these inequalities, but how to achieve conditions of justice which will make possible the maintenance of peace. It is not an easy problem and many people fear it may be too late to apply effective measures for averting the madness of war. The difficulties are enormous. Some of them will be considered when we come to remedies which have been proposed, but two fundamental obstacles must be mentioned here. One arises from the question of power and prestige. As long as the actions of nations are governed by the rule of power politics, and change in the *Status Quo*, the existing condition, inevitably affects the power and prestige of one group or another. Concession to the dissatisfied powers may be shown to be justified but the satisfied power are reluctant to grant such concessions at the point of a gun when they believe that the concession will increase the power of an aggressive Dictator and weaken their own prestige. Yet if no concession is made, the root of conflict is as deep as ever.

The second fundamental difficulty is the fact that at the present time it is not easy to find a legal way by which change can be brought about peacefully. The *World Court*, for the most part, can only hand down legal decisions on the basis of existing international law, but the law of nations is based on treaties and agreements which often do not provide justice or permit Change. Impartial historians agree that the *Versailles Treaty* contained many flagrant injustices, and yet it became the law of Europe after World War I. The League of Nations contains a famous clause, Article 119, which provides for changing treaties, but this article has been voided, and the great powers have used the League to maintain the *Status Quo* rather than to bring about readjustments in the interest of justice and equality.

What is it that the dissatisfied nations say they want? *More Land and Colonies* for increasing populations; raw materials for growing industries; markets for their manufactured goods. The argument advanced by these powers is that the world had been parceled out and the best parts already occupied when they arrived on the scene a modern industrial nations. They feel the pressure of a growing population. They lack necessary raw materials to meet the demands of a higher standard of living for their people. They need territory for expansion and access to essential raw materials and markets to dispose of their manufactured good. They say they do not want *War*, but they demand change and are prepared to take risks in order to gain their ends.

Let us analyze these claims, to see exactly how important or unimportant they are and whether present methods of *(Overcoming)* them are sufficient. In other words, are the dissatisfied nations justified in demanding *change?* If so, how can change be accomplished most satisfactorily for all concerned? The primary need of a people is food. Therefore a nation must be able to grow enough food for its population on its own land, or have raw materials and manufactured goods which it can exchange for food grown in other countries. It is important, therefore, to ask how much land a nation has which can be used for growing crops or raising livestock. Is it enough to supply the existing population and will it continue to be enough to supply the population at is present rate of increase?.

Another point made by some writers is that no government except the Soviet Union actually owns the raw materials in its territory that instead they are owned by private individuals who produce them for profit and are anxious to sell to any one willing to but, whether a citizen or a foreigner; that trade goes on between individuals; and that therefore an analysis of inequalities in the resources of nations is meaningless. It is said, for instance, that British manufacturers must buy and pay for his supply of rubber or oil or cotton, whether it is produced within the British Empire or in the United States. What advantage has he then over the German or the Italian or the Japanese manufacturer?

Finally, it is claimed that regardless of ownership all nations have equal access to raw materials through the channels of international trade. In fact, producers are only too glad to sell to anyone who wants to but. During the world depression, for example, there was tremendous overproduction of all raw materials, so that they were available at very low prices. Japan profited from this state of affairs by buying American cotton below the cost of production and using it in the manufacture of textile which under sold English and American products in many part of the world. There is undoubtedly mush truth is some of these arguments, but they leave a good many pertinent questions unanswered. One might ask, for instance why colonies which are so burdensome are not willingly given up by their present owner? But there are important factors to be considered which these arguments do not take into account and which must be analyzed if the problem of *peaceful change* is to be solved. Other authorities, while not accepting the whole case of the dispossessed power at face value, allow that there grievances which cannot be ignored or dismissed.

In the first place, with regard to migration to colonies, no one can be sure what the future will be. During the nineteenth century there was considerable migration from one country to another. There were continents to be explored, new territories to be settled; frontiers to be opened. As long as people could go to more attractive places to live, where climate, opportunities to work and living conditions were more favorable, it is true they did not go to undeveloped territories where colonization was sure to mean greater hardship. Today, it is said, conditions are different. The doors of practically all the countries to which people from over populated nations migrated in the past have been closed to emigrants. The United States used to receive hundreds of thousands from the crowded nations of Europe every year. Now only a very limited number are allowed to enter. Other nations, including Canada and the countries of South America have passed similar laws restricting immigration. Shut off from these countries, overpopulated nations may turn more readily to less attractive territory. Al though only a few hundred Italians now live in Eritrea or Italian Somaliland, there is no reason to believe that far larger numbers may not migrate to Ethiopia, with the more favorable climate of its high plateau and the assistance of government planning to make colonization more attractive. This does not mean, of course, that the wars of conquest are justified, or that colonies are an answer to the problem.

The extension of mandates to all backward areas would be a better method, if it could be carried out. But the fact remains that old channels of migration have been closed, while the future development of new outlets is unknown. While the balance sheet may not always seem favorable, many private interests in the nations owning colonies undoubtedly profit from the privileged position they enjoy. Then too, colonies serve as an outlet for capital. There can be little doubt that Great Britain has benefited from the exploitation of mines, the building of railroads, and other projects open up in the development of her colonial empire. Although large-scale immigration has been common in Africa and Asia, colonies have furnished opportunities for men from different walks of life, such as trained administrator, engineers, miners, and others. *Another fact which must be taken in account* is that a country's total wealth is determined largely by the extent of its natural resources and the ability of its people to make effective use of them. Given a country with territory rich in resources and *citizens with intelligence* and initiative enough to exploit them, the result will be national *prosperity*. For the wealth produced will tend to raise the living standard of all the people whether is publicly or privately owned. Accumulated capital growing out of the exploitation of natural resources is invested in the production of more and more goods, this in turn means *jobs and wages* and the purchasing power to buy the goods produced. Thus the fact that an American concern owns coal, oil or cotton means that many American citizens share in the return from that resource because it becomes part of the *national economy*.

Furthermore, the government of a nation is organized to protect the interests of its citizens. In the modern industrial world economic interests have become increasingly important. Hence governments have devised a variety of methods to protect their merchants and manufacturers and give them certain advantages over the merchants and manufacturers of other countries. This means that often it is not possible to secure raw materials on as favorable terms from a foreign producer as from a producer at home. Thus natural resources, whether owned by the government or by individuals, are an essential part of the wealth of a nation. And in a nationalistic world each government is eager to do everything it can to conserve and protect the resources within its territory. It is not surprising therefore that nations which are poor in resources see the advantage of owning the raw materials needed for industrialization and are demanding a fairer share of the world's supply. This brings us to what is far the strongest argument in defense of the dissatisfied nations. Granted that raw materials are for sale in the open market, the important fact remains that they may still be beyond the reach of nations which do not have the means to purchase them. It is not enough to say that in this country all people have the same opportunity to procure food and clothing and houses and automobiles imply because producers are willing to sell. Some can afford to buy, others cannot. The matter of ability to buy is just as vital in the case on nations as individuals. In other words, inequalities among nations cannot be wiped out at the present time by means of trade because of certain very real obstacles in the way of free exchange of goods among nations. If nation are to have equal access to raw materials, two things are necessary; those who produce them must be willing to sell at a fair price, and those who wish to buy must have sufficient purchasing power.

Let us pause for a moment to consider the arguments advanced on both sides of this question. It is clear that on one contest the fact that inequalities between nations exist in land, population and resources. It is also reasonable clear that the fortunate powers which build up their colonial empires in the nineteenth century gained certain very real economic benefits. It is not clear that re-division of territory and colonies would remove in equalities or solve the basic problem. Under the system of intense nationalism, such transfers of territory, even if they could be carried out, would be likely to create new inequalities and first grievances in the place of those removed. Here, as we noted earlier, the element of power and prestige becomes and important factor and one which cannot be dealt with as a purely economic problem. It is also a political and military question. But if we are searching for economic solutions and methods of *peaceful change*, we are brought the roux, A cross, an important and critical point, and difficult to explain, the whole problem-the question of trade and markets, and the factor which limit the purchasing power of consumer nations. That demand for change is not likely to stop; countries which believe they have a grievance will not give up their programs of expansion or their desire for colonies unless some better plan can be found. It is vital then, to examine the nature of international trade more carefully than we have done so far. To buy and sell one needs some medium of exchange, In the United States we use dollars, Englishmen use pounds, Frenchmen franks, Germans marks, and so on. As long as trade is carried on within one nation, the business of trade is fairly simple. But buying goods from a merchant in another country is another matter. A German or a Japanese manufacturer desiring to but American cotton or copper cannot send over marks or yen in payment. Before he can place his order, he must secure the necessary dollars in exchange for the currency of his own country. He can do this theoretically by taking his marks or his yens to a bank which deals in foreign exchange. But he will find dollars available at the bank only if an American merchant has been buying goods or services from his country. That is, a merchant can but raw materials only if the producing country is willing to buy foreign goods or services, thus making available the necessary dollars or foreign exchange. In other words, a nation a nation must be willing to trade its goods or services in exchange for the goods or services it wants to buy from other nations. Whether a nation trades as a unit like the Soviet Union, or whether trading is carried on by individual citizens, it is necessary to maintain what is called a balance of trade. If purchases get to far ahead of sales, a nation must ship gold to balance its account, since gold is the standard medium of exchange between nations. But because nations have only a limited supply of gold, trade cannot be carried on long on such a basis. The extremely uneven distribution of gold in the world today, adding to the trade difficulties for the "have-not" nations.

In the final analysis, trade between nations must be an exchange of goods and services. A nation's purchasing power, therefore, is dependent on the free flow of goods. It must be able to buy goods at a fair price and it must have an opportunity to find markets for goods or services it has to sell. In recent years, however, the number of obstacles which have hampered and restricted world trade has increased. The world war disrupted trade and shattered the complex economic machinery of the world. Then rising tariff walls hampered the normal flow of goods across national boundaries. Finally, the great depression, with the collapse of the international banking system led governments to impose new restrictions to protect their currencies and home industries. The effect of all this has been to make it more and more difficult to transact business between nations. It is important therefore, to analyze both the devices to control or limit the supply of raw materials and thus raise prices, and the methods to control markets and prevent the sale of competitive goods. IN addition to preferential tariffs, against various kinds of imported goods, many countries have adopted a system of quotas, under which they place an absolute limit on the amount of a given commodity which is allowed to enter the country. In some countries like France and Czechoslovakia, the quota is allocated among the different producing states on the basis of special bargaining agreements. In other countries the quota applies equally to all states. But the effect under both types of quota is to limit domestic markets and cut down opportunities for foreign trade.

By means of restoring upon a Principle of equality, to return upon a principle of Justice and Honor, to reply unto a Principle of undeniable Right, not always claming what ought to be restored, but only claim and enforce what should be returned or repaid.

This system of government control has been closely identified with the doctrine of economic nationalism.

* * *

PART NINE

THERE IS A
PEACEFUL REMEDY

In considering the proposals which have been advanced, we discover that most impartial experts make a clear distinction between economic remedies which might be applied under a *peace economy* and measures which nations are likely to adopt under a *war economy*. A peace economy, they point out, is judged on the basis of what is required for a decent standard of living; a *war economy is judged* on the basis of military power and potential effectiveness in war. It is important to keep this distinction in mind, for solutions which are capable of meeting purely economic, free from physical or moral defilement, grievances cannot satisfy demands which rest on wartime needs and a *war economy*. This will become clear when we see how to restore and reduce national rearmament programs which have required large imports of raw materials which otherwise would have been unnecessary. It also brings out the close relation between political and military disarmament on the one hand and economic *disarmament* on the other. At the same time, most experts recognize that there is little hope of inducing nations to abandon a *war economy unless legitimate economic grievances are met and definite remedies proposed, with desires, truefully, and honestly acted upon, through harmonious cooperation by those who have been chosen to have authority as representatives of we the people.*

We should not then, confine ourselves to a consideration of our own wretchedness, but rather turn our thoughts to the contemplation of a divine attribute of mercy. Assuredly our faults are displeasing to God, but he does not on their account cease to cherish our souls. It is unnecessary to observe that his applies only to such faults as are due to the frailty inherent in our nature, and against which an upright will, sustained by divine grace, continually struggles. A perverse will, without which there can be no mortal sin, alienates us from God and renders us hateful in His eyes as long as we are subject to it. At the feast spoken of in the *Gospel*, the King receives with *Love* the poor, the blind, and the lame who are clothed with confidence—that is to say, all those whom a desire to please God maintains in a state of grace notwithstanding their natural *defects* and frailty: but his rigorous justice displays itself against him who dares to appear there without this garment. This distinction found everywhere throughout the Gospel is essential in order to inspire us with a tender *confidence* when we fall, without diminishing our horror for deliberate sins. A good mother is affected at the natural defects and infirmity of her child, but she loves him none the less, nor does she refuse him her compassion or her aid. Far from it, for the more miserable and suffering and deformed he may be the greater is her tenderness and solicitude for him. We should not forget our peace of mind by wondering what destiny awaits us in eternity. Our future lot is in the hands of God, and it is much safer there than if in our own keeping. We should be far from allowing ourselves to be dejected by fear and doubt, but raise our desires rather to a greater virtue and to the most sublime perfection. God loves courageous souls. Saint Theresa assures us to mistrust our won strength and place all our reliance upon God. The devil tries to persuade us that it is pride to have exalted aspirations and to wish to imitate the virtues of the saints; but we should not permit him and his followers to deceive us by this artifice. He will only laugh at us if he succeeds by having us to fall into temptation, and that we miss the mark by no exhibiting moral excellence towards godliness, as it is written in scripture, God's sacred holy word that we are to resist him in mind and the devil will flee, as it is written, the battlefield is truly in our minds. If we are tempted, "says the Holy Spirit," it is a sign that God loves us." Those whom God loves best have been most exposed to temptation. "Because thou was acceptable to God," said the angel to Tobias, "it was necessary that temptation should prove thee." We should not ask God to deliver us from temptation, but to grant us the grace not to succumb to them and to do nothing contrary to His divine will. He who refuses the combat, renounces the crown. But we should place all our trust in God His will, God will do battle for us against the enemy.

These persistent temptations come from the malice of the devil, but the trouble and suffering they cause us come from the mercy of God. Thus, despite the will of the temper, God converts his evil machinations into a distress which we may make meritorious. Therefore I say our temptations are from the devil and hell, but our anxiety and affliction are from God and heaven. Despise temptation, then, and open wide our soul to this suffering which God sends in order to purify us here that He may reward us Hereafter. We should look upon God as an infinitely good and tender Father and believe that God only allows the devil to try his children that their merits may increase and their recompense be correspondingly great.

The more persistence the temptation, the clearer it is that we have not given consent to it. When the tempter, the wicked devil spirit makes so much noise and commotion outside of the will, for it shows that he is not within. An enemy does not besiege a fortress that is already in his power, and the more obstinate the attack, the more certain we may be that our resistance continues. Our fears lead us to believe we are defeated at the very moment we are gaining the victory. This comes from the fact that we confound feeling with consent, and mistaking a passive condition of the imagination for an act of the will, we consider that we have yielded to the temptation because we felt it keenly, as a keen edge on a knife.

It is not always in our power to restrain the imagination, the attraction through and feelings become present by our imagination that will lead us to lust, is at times so strong that the will seems to have been carried away and overcome by a sort of fascination. This however, is not the case. The will suffered, but did not consent; it was attacked and wounded, but not conquered. This state of things coincides with what St. Paul says of the revolt of the flesh against the spirit and of their unceasing warfare. The soul indeed, experiences strange sensations, but we do not consent to them, we pass through the ordeal, just as substances coated with oil may be immersed in water without absorbing a single drop of it.

The mental exercising in the mind, of practicing discipline, self control, obedience, is most needful for a believing, obedient Christian today. Ignore therefore, the groundless suspicion that we sin in by obeying, and walk confidently in this path exempt us from danger. We sometimes fear, that in obeying we act against the dictates of our conscience, were as, on the contrary, we really increase our merit before God. We should allow Obedience to regulate not only our exterior actions, but likewise our heart, mind, and our will. In the Holy Bible God's sacred Holy word, says; in the book of Ezekiel 33:31-32, says and they come unto thee as the people cometh, and they sit before thee as my people, and they hear thy words, but they will not do them: for with their mouth they show much love, but their *hearts goeth after their covetousness*, meaning to desire enviously that which belongs to another, discontent, because of the possessions or good fortune of another, dissatisfaction, *lack of contentment, lack of being satisfied with what one has.* We should not just be satisfied with performing the works it prescribes, but let our thoughts and desires be also moulded, in fact, it is this interior submission that the merit of *spiritual obedience essentially consists.*

Obedience should be simple and prompt without reservation, we ought not to argue about it, but decide by the one thought, I must obey, prompt, for it is God whom we are obeying. Because obedience extends to everything that does not violate God's law. Because in obeying God we cannot go astray, (Proverbs 5:22-23, says When thou goest, It shall lead thee: when thou sleepest, it shall keep thee: and when thou awakest, it shall talk with thee. For the commandment is a lamp, and the law is Light: and reproofs of *instruction are the way of life.)* This thought should be sufficient to drive away all fear of doing, or of having done wrong. We should not only be *virtuous, but prudent, and charitable.* The act of *loving kindness*, towards the *poor* and needy and towards our *fellowman, and learned.*

* * *

PART TEN

AN INVITATION
TOWARD CHANGE

I truly believe that change could be a reality when we come to the knowledge that God has Blessed this land that is called America, when we are united as a people and that we choose and desire in our minds and hearts, to be sincere and honest toward one another, meaning, we the people and especially those who has been put in authority to serve our nation by God the creator of us all, and present ourselves before God, giving thanks. Each and everyone of us has a different misery, that needs to be overcome, could it be our *selfish* desires, *egos, conceit-fullness, and greed*, or have we been this way for so long that it has become and acceptable life style, and by this we have allowed ourselves to become automated, human beings un-human creatures stuck in our acceptable character defects. In our nation America, and worldwide, families are stitched with illness unemployment, divorced, separations in every race and nationality as we are classified by those who classify us so that they can play there games of divide and conquer, (like chess) The results is our youth are caught up in frustrations, confusion and out of control, because most of us are un-discipline and out of control, its because we as adults fall short of knowledge, and education on how to raise and train our children to prepare them for adulthood, because we as adults didn't get the training ourselves to pass on to our children. The problem is that discipline and self control is not learned at home or in our school system. We as adults, mentors and role models can't give to the children what is needed if we have never learned discipline and self control ourselves, sadly the end results is too many children fall short, and loose out on life's blessings, of real joy and gladness, we as adults need to get it together so that our children can get it together, then they will have a better chance for prosperity and success and not go astray.

I sincerely believe that the directive given to us from the mind of God, as it is written in God's sacred holy word, the Bible, we should take the time to read and meditate over and over, and read with our children when ever necessary. The book of 2 Timothy, chapter 2: verses 22-26, and teach it to our elementary school children of every nationality and race. Because they are the next leaders of a great need of the new world order, of worldwide peace and brotherly and sisterly love. God invites us to a change of mind and hearts, that is what really should change is the way we feel and think of others, differ in their outward appearances, we should observe other, who even in the face of great adversity manage to lead a balance life and even bring joy unto others in their lives. God's sacred holy word says we are to bring our joy where there is sorrow, and mourning, in order that God may work through these situations to give us peace and joy complete and fulfilled in mind and heart.

* * *

PART ELEVEN

ABOUT THE COVER
And why the Statue of Liberty was chosen

The colossal Statue of Liberty, ingeniously fashioned from hundreds of thin copper plates, was constructed in Paris, France from 1875 to 1884. It was a gift from the people of France to the people of the United States to??-albeit ten years late—the 1876 American Centennial. Originally entitled *"Monument to American Independence Liberty Enlightening the World"* as an acknowledgement of freedom from support by others or from being ruled by others, to whom is granted *Freedom* and the rights to have the Privileges to enjoy life as a symbol of *welcome* to those who are seeking *Liberty*. The statue commemorates the Franco=American alliance and the decisive role France played in the Revolutionary War. But Liberty's creators intended their monument to honor not so much a military victory as a triumph of a heroic social experiment. In a land far removed from monarchies of Europe. The Americans had succeeded in building an enduring republic based on *Liberty and Equality* that had withstood the trials of one hundred years, including a bloody civil war.

For European countries still chafing under the rule of monarchies, or empires, the United States with its Constitution and Bill of Rights provided a potent model of representative government. This was especially true in France where the "Liberte, Fraternite, Egalite" proclaimed by the leaders of the French Revolution in 1789 had in fact remained elusive ideals, frustrated and repressed by a recurring cycle of revolution, anarchy, counter-revolution, and autocracy. Indeed, for Liberty's first patrons, a small group of influential and politically active French intellectuals, the statue paid homage to a form of government—a republic—that they dearly longed to see established in their own country.

Situated dramatically near the center of New York Bay, the gateway to the New World, Liberty soon became a revered and powerful symbol, not just of an abstract ideal, but of America itself. Throughout the past century, generations of Americans have reinterpreted her significance, adapting her image to represent the New concerns and new philosophies of each succeed age. But the special meaning of Liberty for immigrants to the United States—those intrepid *seeking of Liberty* from all over the world—has remained constant from the statue's unveiling today.

* * *

PART TWELVE

PUBLISHER'S
CLOSING COMMENTS

If human mankind would desire and choose in our deepest thoughts and conscience, and in the true fullness of our hearts, and not look at one another judge mentally from our outer appearance, but by our character, attitude and behavior, and understand as the holy scripture saith in 1 Samuel 16:7 "The Lord said to Samuel, look not on his appearance or at the height of his stature, for I have rejected him, for the Lord sees not as man sees, for man looks on the outward appearance, but the Lord looks on the heart." Could it be our extreme thoughts of our inward egos and selfish desires and pride of life, that we have not matured above our childish desires, that we need to overcome, and turn away from myths and lies that have been taught and learned in the years of our childhood that has deceived us all, past and present in mind and heart, and character, leading us to extreme selfish desires of greed and selfish behaviors and immoral thoughts, but righteously and morally, we should be setting a pattern, for the children of the next generation to follow.

But in actuality, we corrupt the minds and morals of our own children, by the chosen *abominable* accepted life styles of our society. We adults have fallen short of knowing who we are and why we are here, *in the eyes of the creator, God.* On the part of being role models and mentors for our children of the next generation Have we become that (vile? I myself would have to say yes. Because in our natural state of mind and heart, we choose to live in selfish life styles selfishly morally and unnecessary, the results is that we are stuck in ruts. And yet we appear to be so in our appearance clean and innocent, but inwardly, we have become inhuman, because we choose not to change our character defects and our wicked ways, and we choose not to give regards to the very God that made us all, and his request is just for us to love one another as he loves us, unconditionally, (not to lust and to become vile, and that we live in harmony as a worldwide brotherhood. When we choose not to live in harmony and at peace, the presents of God is not. If there is no harmony, God is not present, because God will only dwell were there is harmony and love, For God is love.

Through the loving kindness of God we have been blessed, although we have been the recipient of the best that heaven has offered, and we have enjoyed prosperity, wealth, and we have grown in numbers, wealth, success, and power, as no nation has ever grown but we have forgotten God, we have forgotten the hands which has preserved us in peace and enriched us, and we have vainly imagined being caught up in our fantasies, selfish greed, egos and pride, and we have become insatiably greedy, and yet in that state of mind, our extreme thoughts and actions leave us with no fulfillment of true joy and happiness or gladness, we vainly have imagined that our blessings were produced by some superior ungodly wisdom and virtue of our own, that we have become overly intoxicated with unbroken success, and we have become too selfish to feel the necessity and too proud to pray to the God that made us all, and to humble ourselves before the offended power, to confess repent and to pray for forgiveness of our sins. In God's sacred holy word the bible, and proven by all history that those nations that no longer exist, as it is written in the holy scriptures and an historical fact that nations only are blessed whose god is Lord (Psalm 33:12-14) Blessed (happy, fortunate, to be, envied) is the nation whose god is the Lord, the people He has chosen as His heritage. The Lord looks from heaven, He beholds all the sons of men from His dwelling place He Looks intently upon all the inhabitants of the earth—He who fashions the hearts of them all, who considers all their doing (Proverbs 14:340) Uprightness and right standing with God (Moral) and spiritual rectitude in every area and relation elevate a nation, but sin is a reproach, a cause of dishonor or the state of being in dishonor, *to any people.*

* * *

Love

Is patient, love is kind
It does not envy
  It does not boast, it is not proud.
It is not rude, it is not self-seeking,
  It is not easily angered,
It keeps no record of wrongs
  Love does not delight in evil
But rejoices with the truth.
  It always protects, always trust,
  always hopes, always perseveres.
Love never fails. . .
  And now these three remain
    faith, hope and love,
  But the greatest of these is

Love

1 Corinthians 13: 4-13

Love is the Greatest

If I could speak all the languages of earth and of angels, but didn't love others, I would only be a noisy gong or a clanging cymbal. ²If I had the gift of prophecy, and if I understood all of God's secret plans and possessed all knowledge, and if I had such faith that I could move mountains, but didn't love others, I would be nothing. ³If I gave everything I have to the poor and even sacrificed my body, I could boast about it;* but if I didn't love others, I would have gained nothing.

⁴Love is patient and kind. Love is not jealous or boastful or proud ⁵or rude. It does not demand its own way. It is not irritable, and it keeps no record of being wronged. ⁶It does not rejoice about injustice but rejoices whenever the truth wins out. ⁷Love never gives up, never loses faith, is always hopeful, and endures through every circumstance.

⁸Prophecy and speaking in unknown languages* and special knowledge will become useless. But love will last forever! ⁹Now our knowledge is partial and incomplete, and even the gift of prophecy reveals only part of the whole picture! ¹⁰But when full understanding comes, these partial things will become useless. 1 CORINTHIANS 13.

¹¹When I was a child, I spoke and thought and reasoned as a child. But when I grew up, I put away childish things. ¹²Now we see things imperfectly as in a cloudy mirror, but then we will see everything with perfect clarity.* All that I know now is partial and incomplete, but then I will know everything completely, just as God now knows me completely.

¹³Three things will last forever—faith, hope, and love—and the greatest of these is love.

Joy Complete
Have the Attitude of Christ

If, therefore, in relationship with Christ there is any encouragement. If there is any fellowship in the Spirit, If any affections and compassion, then make my joy complete by being in agreement having the same love being united in spirit, having the same attitude, doing nothing out of selfishness or conceit, but with humility regarding others superior to yourselves. Neither must each be looking out only for how own interests but also for those of others. Let this mind be in you which was also in Christ Jesus.

Philippians 2:1-5

Suggested Readings Colossians 3:8-14

The highest reward for our work is not what we get for it. But what we become by it.

MINISTER F. IRVING PEARSALL

*Love worketh no ill to his neighbour,
therefore love is the fulfilling of the law.*

11 And that, knowing the time, that now it is high time to awake out of sleep: for now is our salvation nearer than when we believed. Mark 13:37

12 The night is far spent, the day is at hand: let us therefore cast off the works of darkness, and let us put on the armour of light.

13 Let us walk honestly, as in the day, not in rioting and drunkenness, not in chambering and wantonness, not in strife and envying.

14 But put ye on the Lord Jesus Christ, and make not provision for the flesh, to fulfill the lusts thereof. Romans 13

SUGGESTED READINGS
Matthew 22:37-40

The Prayer For Peace

*A Prayer for The President of the United States,
and all in Civil Authority*

ALMIGHTY God, whose kingship is everlasting and power intense. Have mercy upon this whole body and so rule the hearts of thy servants, THE PRESIDENT OF THE UNITED STATES, The Governor of this State, and all others in authority, that they, knowing whose ministers they are, may above all things seek thy honour and glory, and that we and all the People, duly considering whose authority they bear, may faithfully and obediently honour them, according to thy blessed Word and ordinance; through Jesus Christ our Lord, who with thee and the Holy Ghost liveth and reigneth ever, one God, world without end. Amen.

FOR OUR NATION

ALMIGHTY God, who hast given us this good land for our heritage; We humbly beseech thee that we may always prove ourselves a people mindful of thy favour and glad to do thy will. Bless our land with honourable industry, sound learning, and pure manners. Save us from violence, discord, and confusion; from pride and arrogance, and from every evil way. Defend our liberties, and fashion into the united people the multitudes brought hither out of many hundreds and tongues. Endure with the spirit of wisdom those to whom in thy Name we entrust the authority of government, that there may be justice and peace at home, and that, through obedience to thy Law, we may show forth thy praise among the nations of the earth. In the time of the prosperity, fill our hearts with thankfulness, and in the day of trouble, suffer not our trust in thee to fail; all which we ask through Jesus Christ our Lord. Amen.